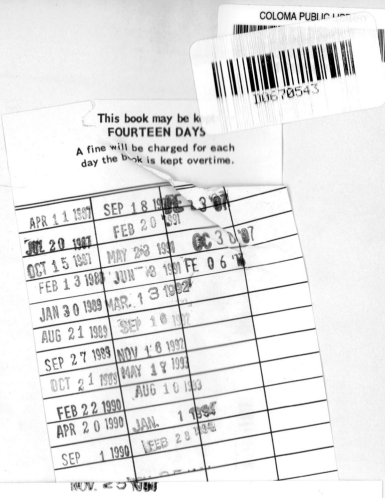

# FOOT-FIGHTING
## MANUAL
## FOR SELF-DEFENSE AND
## SPORT KARATE

Fred Neff's Self-Defense Library

# FOOT-FIGHTING
## MANUAL
## FOR SELF-DEFENSE AND
## SPORT KARATE

Fred Neff

Photographs by James E. Reid

Lerner Publications Company
Minneapolis

The models photographed in this book are Bruce Bottomley, Mike Podolinsky, Bill Polta, and Laura Phillips.

LIBRARY OF CONGRESS CATALOGING IN PUBLICATION DATA

**Neff, Fred.**
Foot-fighting manual for self-defense and sport karate.

(Fred Neff's Self-Defense Library)
SUMMARY: Explains the use of the feet in self-defense and competition karate and demonstrates both basic and advanced techniques.

1. Self-defense. 2. Karate. [1. Self-defense. 2. Karate] I. Reid, James E. II. Title.

GV1111.N44 1977            796.8'153            75-38474
ISBN 0-8225-1153-3

Manufactured in the United States of America

International Standard Book Number: 0-8225-1153-3
Library of Congress Catalog Card Number: 75-38474

4   5   6   7   8   9   10   90   89   88   87   86   85   84

# CONTENTS

*To Bruce Bottomley, Bill Polta, and Mike Podolinsky, who have shown great loyalty and devotion to their instructor and their martial art*

# PREFACE

When I became a student of karate in the 1950's, few Americans had knowledge of the Oriental fighting arts or were interested in learning them. Since that time, however, public interest in the subject has grown considerably. Today, thousands of people all over the country are studying the various fighting arts and are learning that they offer many physical, psychological, and social benefits.

This new interest and involvement in the Oriental fighting arts has created a need for books that can be used as instructional guides for beginning students. FRED NEFF'S SELF-DEFENSE LIBRARY was written to help meet that need. My purpose in writing the series was to provide a basic comprehensive course on self-defense, based on the major Oriental disciplines of karate, judo, and jujitsu. In preparing each book, I was careful to include not only the physical techniques of Oriental fighting but also the underlying philosophical principles. This is important because an understanding of both elements is required of every martial arts student. Finally, in selecting the particular self-defense techniques for each book, I tried to include techniques that could be of practical use to the average person and that could be performed effectively and safely through practice. I genuinely hope that each and every reader of the SELF-DEFENSE LIBRARY benefits as much as I have from studying the martial arts.

Fred Neff

# INTRODUCTION

In the United States and in most other countries of the world, people usually use their hands to defend themselves in a fight. In some parts of the world, however—especially in Asia—people also use their feet. In fact, certain Chinese, Japanese, and Korean systems of self-defense are based primarily on foot techniques.

There are several advantages to using the feet for fighting. In the first place, the human leg is strong, so kicking is a very powerful technique. Secondly, because the human leg is a long limb, a kick can be delivered to any part of the body. A third advantage of foot fighting is that it involves the element of surprise. Aggressors do not expect to defend against foot techniques, so they are often caught off guard by kicks, foot sweeps, and leg throws.

Though foot-fighting techniques are dramatic maneuvers, beginning self-defense students should remember that there is nothing magical about performing them. This must be emphasized because movies and television shows often present a distorted view of how foot-fighting techniques are used and performed. The goal of such productions, of course, is not to teach but to entertain the viewers and to arouse an emotional response in them. It is important that self-defense students recognize this and do not take such portrayals seriously or copy them. The only way that a person can effectively use self-defense techniques is through dedicated study and practice of authentic Asian fighting techniques.

This book has been written to teach the Oriental art of foot fighting for self-defense and sport karate. Because each chapter acts as a foundation for the next, it is important to take the chapters in sequence and to learn each technique in order. As a beginning self-defense student, you should practice the techniques until you can do them automatically. In accomplishing that, you will gain a great deal of confidence in your ability to defend yourself from physical attack.

# COMMON QUESTIONS ON FOOT FIGHTING

Beginning self-defense students always have many questions about foot-fighting techniques and about sport karate. The questions that are asked most frequently include the six that appear in this chapter.

**1. What kinds of techniques are included in foot fighting for self-defense?**

The basic foot-fighting techniques include kicks, foot sweeps, and leg throws. In addition to these, students should also learn the various dodging and blocking techniques.

**2. Can I defend myself successfully by using foot techniques alone?**

If you were attacked, it would be possible for you to defend yourself with foot techniques and nothing else. But your defense would be stronger and more effective if you used hand techniques too. Even kicking experts would find themselves at a disadvantage if they used only foot techniques in a fight. It is important, therefore, that students of self-defense learn to use hand techniques as well as foot techniques. In self-defense situations, it is the student's coordination in executing a variety of moves that makes his or her defense effective.

**3. Should I always try to use head-level kicks in a fight?**

Head-level kicks, or those directed at the head and upper chest areas, are too difficult for beginning students to use effectively. This is because they are easily blocked and often leave the defender open to being thrown off balance by the attacker. Even kicking experts are reluctant to throw head-level kicks in a real fight. They do it only if there are no other openings on the attacker. Head-level kicks are used most often in sport karate tournaments, where a person can win a match by kicking at—but not striking—the opponent's head.

The best kicks to use in an actual fight are the lower-level kicks, or those thrown to the stomach, groin, knees, and feet. These kicks are thrown with a great deal of power and are the ones most likely to stop an attacker.

**4. What are the goals of sport karate?**

The goals of sport karate are the development of character and self-control, and the improvement of physical fitness and self-defense abilities.

Character is developed through the challenge of competition, which forces participants to defend themselves while practicing good sportsmanship. In addition to developing character, participants learn to increase their self-control. Tournament rules, which limit the amount of physical force that can be used at a given time, usually call for blows to stop at least one inch (2.5 centimeters) from target areas. Furthermore, rules do not allow participants to insult or provoke one another.

Still another benefit of karate competition is that its participants become physically fit from practicing self-defense techniques. Karate competitors are also better able to defend themselves in real-life self-defense situations.

## 5. What is a sport karate tournament?

A sport karate tournament usually involves two competitors who try to score points by throwing blows that stop at least one inch (2.5 centimeters) from the target. To count as a point, a blow must be well executed and controlled. It must be done with good form and without interference, or blocking, by the opponent. In an actual competition, four judges and one referee decide whether a blow is "delivered" well enough to count as a point.

Karate tournaments generally do not call for violent physical contact. Tournament rules declare each match a sporting event, and officials are always present to enforce the rules. Some tournaments require competitors to use safety equipment.

A few tournaments, however, allow a great deal of physical contact. These tournaments have their own sets of rules. Karate instructors and students should request tournament rules far in advance to determine what kind of match they are entering.

## 6. What are the basic principles of karate for students of self-defense?

—A karate person should practice self-control at all times.

—A karate person should never use a fighting technique against another person unless he or she is in danger of being physically harmed.

—A karate person should always remember that along with increased strength and skill in fighting goes a greater responsibility to show kindness and respect toward others.

# 1.

## EXERCISES FOR FOOT FIGHTING

Every day we use our hands and arms for many different tasks. But we do not usually use our feet and legs for any activity other than walking or running. As a result, our legs and feet are not as well conditioned as our arms and hands. That is why students of foot fighting must exercise these parts of their bodies. Along with special foot-fighting exercises, of course, general calisthenics should also be done.

The exercises in this chapter are designed to condition your legs for foot fighting. It is recommended that you practice each exercise several times before you practice the various foot-fighting techniques. When exercising, do not stretch your muscles too much during a practice session. Remember that it is far better to do a little stretching each day and improve slowly than to exercise too much and injure muscles.

### Front Bending Exercise

From an erect stance, bend over and touch the palms of your hands against the ground without bending your knees.

# Leg Stretching Exercise

Standing in a relaxed position with your feet together, kick one leg and then the other straight up without bending your knees. To get the best results from this exercise, kick as high as possible.

# Leg Swing Exercise

Spread your legs far apart, with one leg slightly ahead of the other. Extend the opposite arm out to the side of your body, palm facing forward. Swing the front leg across to the extended hand, hitting it with the sole of your foot. This exercise will condition your body for the crescent kick, which is shown in Chapter 6.

## Sit-Up Exercise

Lie flat on the ground with your hands at your sides. Sit up and touch your toes. Lie down again and repeat the exercise several times. Sit-ups will strengthen your stomach muscles and make your spinal column more flexible.

## Body Twisting Exercise

Spread your legs apart, bend your knees, and extend your arms straight out to either side of your body. Then, twist at the waist as far as you can in each direction.

## Leaping Exercise

Squat on the ground and clasp your hands behind your back. Pushing from your toes, leap into the air as high as you can. This exercise will condition your body for the flying side kick, which is shown in Chapter 6.

## Basic Flexibility Exercise

From a relaxed standing position, slowly spread your legs as far apart as possible. It is recommended that you learn this exercise gradually so that you don't stretch your muscles too much during any one practice session.

## Toes-Up Leg Stretch

This exercise and the following one must be done with a partner. Place one foot, toes up, on the shoulder of your partner, who is in a bent-knee position. Your partner should slowly rise to a standing position while maintaining a firm grip on your leg. As your partner rises, your leg muscles will stretch.

## Toes-To-The-Side Leg Stretch

Place the side of your foot on the shoulder of your partner, who is in a bent-knee position. Your knee and toes should be pointing to the side. Your partner should slowly rise to a standing position while maintaining a firm grip on your leg. As your partner rises, the muscles of your leg and the side of your body will stretch.

# SPECIAL FALLING EXERCISES

One of the most important things for a beginning self-defense student to learn is how to fall safely. Knowing how to fall will keep you from being injured if you are thrown during a fight. It will also build your self-confidence, for if you know that you can fall without being hurt, you will no longer fear being thrown to the ground. For these reasons, you should learn and practice the basic falling exercises presented here. As you practice, be sure to remember these essential points:

1. Always practice the falling exercises on a large, thick mat.

2. The best time to practice the falling exercises is right after the regular warm-up exercises, when your body is loose and flexible.

## The Back Fall Exercise

This fall can be used when you are thrown or tripped so that you fall directly backward.

### Learning Steps

**1.** Start in a squatting position with your knees deeply bent. Extend your arms directly in front of your body, and tuck in your chin.

**2.** Allow your body to fall back, raising your arms as you fall. Be sure to keep your chin securely tucked in. This will prevent your head from hitting the mat when you land.

**3.** Just before your back touches the mat, break your fall by slapping your forearms against the mat about six inches (15 centimeters) from either side of your body.

**4.** When you have completed the fall, your body should be in the position shown in the last photo.

# The Side Fall Exercise

This falling technique is a very effective means of avoiding injury when you are thrown over an opponent's hip or shoulder. You can also use this fall when you are tripped, or when you are thrown by a leg sweep.

## Learning Steps

**1.** Start in a squatting position, with one leg crossed just in front of the other.

**2.** Gradually slide your front leg forward. This sliding action should cause you to lose your balance and to fall on your side. As you fall, bring your arm up in the air.

**3.** Just before you hit the mat, beat the palm of your raised hand against the mat to break your fall.

**4.** It is very important that your body land properly so that knees, ankles, and other sensitive areas are not injured. Make sure that after you land, your body is in the position illustrated in the last photo.

# 2.

## SENSITIVE AREAS OF THE BODY

The human leg can be a very powerful weapon when used to kick an aggressor. But strength alone cannot make a kick an effective self-defense technique; a kick must stop an aggressor's attack in order to be of any value. For this reason, students of foot fighting are taught to kick the particularly sensitive areas of an aggressor's body. These sensitive areas are more vulnerable to pain and are more easily damaged than other areas of the body. A strong kick to any sensitive area will quickly stop an attacker from making any more aggressive moves.

Through the use of charts and diagrams, this chapter shows the body's most sensitive areas and explains which foot techniques can be used most effectively against those sensitive areas. Also included is a picture of the foot, showing the main kicking areas.

# Sensitive Areas of the Body

**Front view**

**Back view**

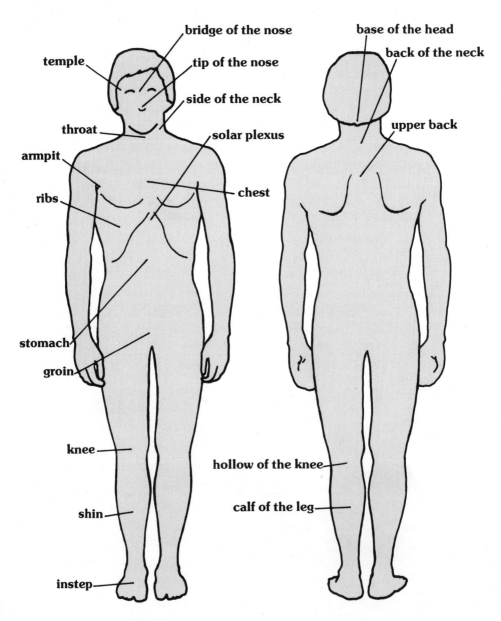

Front view labels:
- bridge of the nose
- temple
- tip of the nose
- side of the neck
- throat
- solar plexus
- armpit
- chest
- ribs
- stomach
- groin
- knee
- shin
- instep

Back view labels:
- base of the head
- back of the neck
- upper back
- hollow of the knee
- calf of the leg

# Sensitive Body Areas and Corresponding Kicking Techniques

## Front of the body

**Temple.** . . . . . . . . . . . . . . . . Round kick, crescent kick, back-spinning circle kick

**Bridge of the nose.** . . . . . . . Front kick, basic side kick, knee kick, any flying kick

**Tip of the nose.** . . . . . . . . . . Front kick, basic side kick, knee kick, any flying kick

**Throat.** . . . . . . . . . . . . . . . . Front kick, basic side kick, knee kick

**Side of the neck.** . . . . . . . . . Round kick, back-spinning circle kick, any flying kick

**Chest.** . . . . . . . . . . . . . . . . . Round kick, front kick, back kick, basic side kick, knee kick, back-spinning circle kick, spinning side kick, any flying kick

**Armpit.** . . . . . . . . . . . . . . . . Front kick, basic side kick

**Solar plexus.** . . . . . . . . . . . . Round kick, basic side kick, front kick, advancing heel kick, any flying kick

**Ribs.** . . . . . . . . . . . . . . . . . . Front kick, basic side kick, round kick

**Stomach.** . . . . . . . . . . . . . . . Round kick, front kick, back kick, side kicks, knee kick, back-spinning circle kick, spinning side kick, ground kicks, any flying kick

**Groin.** . . . . . . . . . . . . . . . . . Front kick, side kicks, back kicks, knee kicks, ground kicks

**Knee.** . . . . . . . . . . . . . . . . . Front kick, stamping kick, basic side kick, ground kicks

**Shin.** . . . . . . . . . . . . . . . . . . Front kick, stamping kick

**Instep.** . . . . . . . . . . . . . . . . Stamping kick

## Back of the body

**Base of the head.** . . . . . . . . Back-spinning circle kick, front kick

**Back of the neck.** . . . . . . . . Back-spinning circle kick, front kick

**Upper back.** . . . . . . . . . . . . . Front kick, basic side kick

**Hollow of the knee.** . . . . . . . Front kick, stamping kick, side kicks

**Calf of the leg.** . . . . . . . . . . . Front kick, stamping kick

# Areas of the Foot Used for Kicking

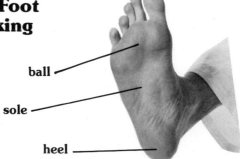

ball

sole

heel

# 3.

## STANCES FOR FOOT FIGHTING

It is impossible to master the techniques of foot fighting without first developing strong fighting *stances*. Stances are special body positions from which the various dodges and blocks, and hand and foot techniques are performed. In a self-defense situation, the person who can quickly position himself or herself in a strong stance will be able to make a good defensive move.

The greatest advantage of having a strong fighting stance is that it provides a great deal of physical stability. This is important because an aggressor will always try to take advantage of a person's weak body position by throwing him or her off balance. The person who assumes a strong stance, however, cannot be thrown off balance.

Physical stability, in turn, enables a person to dodge or block an aggressor's attack more easily. A primary goal of effective self-defense is to always maintain a secure body position so that an attack can be blocked and a counterattack made. A strong fighting stance will make this possible.

Along with a strong fighting stance also goes a feeling of self-confidence. This self-confidence not only enables a person to fight more effectively, but it also makes an aggressor reluctant to attack. Generally, an aggressor will not attack a person who is not afraid to fight.

This chapter presents the basic fighting stances. Practice each stance until you can do all of them automatically. You should also practice moving from one stance to another quickly with smooth, graceful motions; this will help you move effectively in a real self-defense situation.

# The Horse Stance

This stance is very flexible because you can easily move from it to any of the other fighting stances. It can be used for either defense or counterattack. When you practice the horse stance, maintain the stance for several minutes in order to strengthen your leg muscles for fighting.

## Learning Steps

**1.** Spread your legs apart and bend your knees as though you were riding a horse.

**2.** Point your toes inward toward the opening between your legs.

**3.** Make fists of your hands and hold them, palms up, slightly above your hips.*

**4.** Keep the upper half of your body erect, and make sure that your body weight is distributed evenly between both legs.

*NOTE: A proper fist is made by folding your fingers tightly into your palm and by placing your thumb across your forefinger. Keep in mind that there are many different ways to hold the hands in the various fighting stances. Generally, however, it is best to keep both hands at waist level with at least one of them in a fist.

# The Modified Horse Stance

The modified horse stance is the most commonly used stance in foot fighting. Any dodge, block, kick, or leg throw can be done from this stance.

## Learning Steps

**1.** Spread your legs apart as in the horse stance, but do not face your attacker straight on.

**2.** Keep the upper half of your body erect and your knees bent. Your body weight should be evenly distributed between both legs.

**3.** Hold one hand above your hip in the palm-up fist position. Keep the other hand open, palm down, and extend it forward.

## The Basic Back Stance

The back stance is used primarily for defense. You should practice this stance so that you can shift quickly into it if you are attacked. From a back stance position you can easily throw a front kick, a powerful foot technique described in Chapter 6.

### Learning Steps

**1.** Place one leg in front of the other so that your feet are spread apart about twice the width of your shoulders.

**2.** The rear leg should be bent deeply and should carry about 70 percent of your body weight. The front leg should carry 30 percent of your weight.

**3.** Hold one hand above your hip in the palm-up fist position. Keep the other hand open, palm down, and extend it forward.

## The Cat Stance

The cat stance is used for throwing very powerful front kicks.

### Learning Steps

**1.** Stand with one leg directly in front of the other.

**2.** The rear leg should be planted firmly on the ground with the knee slightly bent and facing to the side. It should carry most of your body weight.

**3.** The front leg should be bent at the knee and balanced lightly on the ball of the foot. In this position it is free for throwing very fast kicks.

**4.** Both hands should be made into fists and carried at your sides.

# 4.

# BASIC BODY MOVEMENTS FOR FOOT FIGHTING

In order to use Asian foot-fighting techniques effectively, you will need to know how to move your body in both defense and attack situations. Stability and balance must be maintained at all times, even while you are moving.

## The Basic Sliding Technique

Sliding is the best technique for covering short distances quickly. You can move forward, backward, or diagonally by sliding. Sliding can be done from the modified horse stance, the forward guarding stance, and the basic back stance.

### Learning Steps

**1.** Slide one foot forward or backward, and allow the other foot to follow.

**2.** Maintain your fighting stance and your balance as you slide forward or backward.

# The Basic Stepping Technique

Stepping forward or backward is one of the most common movements in fighting. The advantage of stepping is that it allows you to cover a fairly large distance quickly.

## Learning Steps

**1.** Lift the stepping foot off the ground only slightly. Quickly move the foot forward or backward and set it down.

**2.** Make sure that the other foot, which serves as a pivot, is planted firmly on the ground. Proper posture and balance must be maintained throughout the movement.

## Cross-Stepping

Cross-stepping is used for moving to the right or the left and for covering large distances quickly. It is a movement that actually allows you to take a double step. Cross-stepping often confuses an aggressor, making it difficult for him or her to understand what you are going to do next. Cross-stepping is done most successfully from either the horse stance or the modified horse stance.

### Learning Steps

**1.** When moving to the left, lift your right foot and move it to the other side of your left foot. At this point, your knees should be bent and your feet crossed.

**2.** In a continuing motion, move the left foot around behind the right foot and take a large step farther to the left.

**3.** When moving to the right, reverse these movements.

## The Basic Circling Technique

This method of movement is best done from the modified horse stance.

### Learning Steps

**1.** From your stance, move the front foot four to eight inches (10 to 20 centimeters) to the right or the left, depending on which direction you want to go.

**2.** Once the front foot has been moved, use it as a pivot to swing the rest of the body in the desired direction. In completing the pivot, make sure that the rear foot is planted firmly on the ground. After completing this two-step method, you should again be in a strong fighting stance.

NOTE: The pictures illustrate a basic circling technique in which the model took his first step to the left and then used his stepping foot to swing the rest of his body to the left. If the model had wanted to move to the right, he would have stepped to the right with his front foot and used that foot to pivot the rest of his body to the right.

# 5.

## DODGES AND BLOCKS FOR HAND AND FOOT ATTACKS

Part of every student's self-defense training is to learn how to dodge and block an attack. This is important because in a self-defense situation it is not enough to know how to punch and kick. If a person doesn't know how to avoid being hit, he or she may never get the chance to counterattack.

This chapter is designed to teach students how to dodge and block an aggressor's attack. Included in the chapter are techniques for deflecting both hand and foot attacks. It is best to practice the techniques slowly at first until you become familiar with them. When you feel that you can do them well, speed up your movements. You should eventually be able to perform each dodge and block almost automatically. As you practice, try to imagine that you are defending yourself from an actual attack. You might also find it helpful to practice in front of a mirror. That way, you can compare your body movements with those of the models in the photographs. Another idea is to practice the dodges and blocks with a partner. This will give you the best idea of what it is like to handle an attack.

# DODGING TECHNIQUES

## The Downward Dodge

This dodge is very useful for evading kicks to the chest and stomach. It can be done only from the modified horse stance.

### Learning Steps

**1.** Position yourself in the modified horse stance.

**2.** As the kick is thrown, smoothly shift your weight back to your rear leg, bending it at the knee so that your body is out of range of the attack. Keep your front leg straight, and bring your rear arm up to protect your head.

**3.** When the aggressor's leg fails to make contact with your body, it will lose a great deal of power. This will make it easy for you to push the leg away. To do this, shift your weight forward again and push the leg away with your forward hand. Doing this will break the person's balance and will cause him or her to fall.

## Dodging to the Side

Dodging to the side of a punch is an excellent self-defense technique. It is a good method to use when you are not in a fighting stance but are standing normally with your feet together. Use this dodge when a punch is being thrown at your neck or your head.

### Learning Steps

**1.** As the aggressor releases the punch, bend the upper part of your body to one side. If you move to the left, bring your left hand up to shield your face in case you don't dodge quickly enough. If you dodge to the right, bring your right hand up.

**2.** Be sure to shift your weight in the direction you are bending so that you can maintain proper balance.

# BLOCKING TECHNIQUES

## The Upper-Level Block

This technique is used to block attacks to the head and upper chest area. The upper-level block can be done from any of the fighting stances.

### Learning Steps

**1.** As the aggressor throws the punch, bring your arm upward. The top of your forearm should come in contact with the soft underside of the aggressor's forearm.

**2.** Your blocking arm should deflect the blow upward, away from your body.

# The Mid-Level Block

The mid-level block is useful for protecting yourself from punches to the lower chest and stomach. This block can be done from any of the fighting stances.

## Learning Steps

**1.** As the aggressor releases the punch, bring your front arm up from its lowered position with a strong snapping motion.

**2.** Meet the attacker's blow with the hard inside edge of your forearm. Your blocking arm must be bent sharply at the elbow to withstand the force of the attacker's blow.

## The Crescent Block

This block is a foot technique that is used to protect against hand attacks to the lower chest and stomach. It is done most often from the modified horse stance.

### Learning Steps

**1.** Start from the modified horse stance, as shown in Figure 1.

**2.** When the aggressor throws the punch, swing your rear leg around to the front of your body and deflect the blow with the sole of your foot. Be sure to turn your toes upward to avoid injury.

**3.** After blocking the attack, quickly return your leg to its fighting stance position so that proper balance is maintained.

# The Lower-Level Block

The lower-level block is extremely useful for blocking attacks to the stomach and groin. It can be done successfully from any of the fighting stances.

## Learning Steps

**1.** As the attacker throws the punch or kick, bring your blocking arm up to the opposite ear. At the same time, extend the other arm downward to protect the stomach and groin.

**2.** To block the attack, swing the blocking arm downward so that the outside edge of your forearm meets the attacker's punch or kick.

**3.** Then quickly bring the lowered arm up to the hip in a palm-up fist position. This will prepare you to counterattack, if necessary.

# The Low Cross Block

The low cross block is very effective for stopping front kicks aimed at the lower body regions. This block can be done easily from any of the fighting stances.

## Learning Steps

**1.** From your fighting stance, cross your fists at the wrists and extend them down in front of your body to meet the attack.

**2.** The aggressor's kick should be caught between your two fists.

# 6.

# KICKING TECHNIQUES

This chapter contains the various foot techniques used in kicking. Mastery of these techniques is perhaps the most difficult part of self-defense training. A great deal of hard work and practice is required of students who want to become skilled at kicking.

The best students display proper *form* in their kicking techniques. This means that each movement is done correctly, with good timing and physical coordination. Maintaining proper form is the only way that a student can execute strong, effective kicks. When performed well, these kicks can be effective moves for both sport karate tournaments and self-defense.

Students can practice their kicking form with one another, but they should not actually make contact. When practicing the *impact* of their kicks, students should use a punching bag. The only time a kick should actually be used against another person is in a real self-defense situation.

# BEGINNING KICKS

## The Basic Front Kick

The front kick is a powerful foot technique used for counterattack. It is used most often to strike an aggressor's shins, knees, groin, chest, or head.

### Learning Steps

**1.** Start from a normal standing position, with your feet together.

**2.** Bend the knee of your kicking leg and lift it toward your chest. Turn the toes upward so they will not be injured when your foot hits the target.

**3.** Snap the kicking leg forward and hit your target with the ball of your foot.

# The Basic Side Kick

The basic side kick is an especially powerful technique for counter-attack. It can be used against the knees, groin, stomach, or head of an aggressor.

## Learning Steps

**1.** Stand in a relaxed position, with your feet together.

**2.** Lift the kicking leg and hold it next to the supporting leg, bent at the knee. Be sure that your toes are turned upward.

**3.** Thrust the kicking leg out to the side of your body, and hit the target with the heel of your foot.

**4.** These steps should be practiced until the kick can be done with a single powerful thrusting motion.

## The Basic Back Kick

The back kick is used to defend against attacks from the rear. It is very important to maintain proper balance throughout the back kick so that you will have enough power to stop an aggressor.

## Learning Steps

**1.** Start from the modified horse stance.

**2.** Bring your rear leg forward and lift it toward your chest. At the same time, turn your head so that you can see behind you.

**3.** Thrust the kicking leg straight back, and strike your target with the heel of your foot.

**4.** When the target has been hit, return your leg to the bent-knee position. If there is no need to throw additional kicks, return to the stance position.

# The Basic Ground Kick

This technique enables a person on the ground to fight off an aggressor who is standing. A properly executed ground kick often catches an aggressor by surprise because he or she does not expect the downed person to keep on fighting.

## Learning Steps

**1.** From your position on the ground, draw your knees toward your chest. Your feet should be facing the attacker, and your hands should be flat against the ground, bracing your body.

**2.** Thrust one leg and then the other toward the aggressor's shins, knees, groin, or stomach. Hit with either the heel or the ball of your foot, depending upon the area you are aiming at and your distance from the aggressor.

**3.** Do not get off the ground until the aggressor has retreated. Be prepared to use hand techniques if your foot technique has not stopped the attack.

## The Stamping Kick

The stamping kick is a useful technique for striking the knees, shins, or feet of an aggressor. It can also be used to distract an aggressor so that a middle-level or high-level body punch can be thrown without being blocked.

## Learning Steps

**1.** From a normal standing position, raise the kicking leg toward your chest.

**2.** Thrust the kicking leg downward so that your heel strikes the target.

## The Crescent Kick

The crescent kick is an excellent technique for striking an aggressor's ribs and chest in counterattack. This kick can also be used for blocking an aggressor's hand attacks.

### Learning Steps

**1.** From your stance, bring your rear leg forward and strike the aggressor with the sole of your foot.

**2.** Remember to turn your toes upward so they will not be injured when you kick.

# The Knee Kick

The knee kick is used for striking an aggressor who is standing directly in front of you. It is an effective technique for striking the stomach or groin of an attacker.

## Learning Steps

**1.** Stand in a relaxed position, with your feet together.

**2.** Bring your knee up sharply and hit the aggressor in the stomach or groin.

## The Round Kick

The round kick will surprise an attacker because it will hit where it is least expected—on the side of the body. This kick is especially suited for attacking an aggressor's head, neck, or ribs.

### Learning Steps

**1.** Start from a fighting stance. Figure 1 shows the modified horse stance.

**2.** Shift your weight to the front leg and swing your back leg around toward the attacker. The leg should be bent at the knee and held away from your body, parallel to the ground.

**3.** As your leg swings around the side of your body, snap the kicking leg outward and hit your target with the ball of your foot.

**4.** After striking the target, return your leg to the bent-knee position. If there is no need to throw additional kicks, return to your stance position.

## INTERMEDIATE KICKS

### The Advancing Side Kick

This powerful kick can be used on an aggressor who is standing out of range of the basic side kick.

### Learning Steps

**1.** Start in the horse stance, with the side of your body and your kicking leg facing the aggressor.

**2.** Next, bring your rear leg over your kicking leg so that your feet are crossed.

**3.** Then bring the kicking leg around in front again and raise it toward your chest in a bent-knee position.

**4.** Thrust the kicking leg out to the side of your body and hit the aggressor with the heel of your foot.

## The Spinning Side Kick

The spinning side kick is an unusual technique that often catches an attacker by surprise. This kick is most often used to strike an aggressor's stomach or chest.

### Learning Steps

**1.** Start from a horse stance with the side of your body facing the aggressor.

**2.** Pivot on your front foot and swing your body *backward* toward the aggressor.

**3.** As your body spins around, bend your kicking leg at the knee and turn your head so that you can see the attacker over your shoulder.

**4.** When you can see your target, thrust your kicking leg out to the side of your body and hit the aggressor with the heel of your foot.

## The Advancing Heel Kick

This is a very powerful kick for striking an aggressor's groin, stomach, chest, or head.

### Learning Steps

**1.** Start from a modified horse stance, with the side of your body and your kicking leg facing the aggressor.

**2.** Bring your rear foot behind your kicking leg. The inside edge of your rear foot should rest near or against the heel of your kicking foot.

**3.** Bring your kicking leg toward your chest in a bent-knee position, facing away from the aggressor. Your head should be turned in the direction of the attack.

**4.** Thrust the kicking leg straight back and hit the aggressor with the heel of your foot.

# The Flying Front Kick

Use this technique for striking an aggressor who is out of range of the basic front kick. The flying front kick is used for striking the head and chest of an aggressor.

## Learning Steps

**1.** Start from a modified horse stance, as shown in Figure 1.

**2.** Bring your rear leg forward and jump high into the air.

**3.** Thrust your front leg forward and hit the target with the sole of your foot.

## The Back Kick With Arm Support

This technique will help you defend yourself from an aggressor who is behind you. It can be used to attack the aggressor's groin or stomach.

### Learning Steps

**1.** Start from a normal standing position with your feet together.

**2.** Bend forward and place both hands on the ground for support.

**3.** Move one leg forward, bringing the knee to your chest. Then sharply thrust the leg directly backward and kick the aggressor with the heel of your foot.

## The Side Kick From the Ground

This kick should be used if an aggressor throws you to the ground and continues to attack. You can use this technique to strike the aggressor's knees, groin, or lower stomach.

## Learning Steps

**1.** Position yourself so that you are lying on your side. For support, place the palms of your hands against the ground, one on either side of your body.

**2.** Bend your knees deeply and draw them toward your chest.

**3.** Thrust the top leg straight out to the side so that your heel hits the aggressor's knees, groin, or lower stomach.

# ADVANCED KICKS

## The Flying Side Kick

The flying side kick can be used for hitting an aggressor's upper body. It is a dramatic technique that is executed from the side of the body.

### Learning Steps

**1.** Start from the horse stance. Be sure to look in the direction that you are going to kick.

**2.** Leap high into the air, drawing both legs close to the body.

**3.** Thrust the leg closest to the aggressor straight out to the side. Make sure that the other foot is drawn up close to the kicking leg.

**4.** Strike the target with the heel of your kicking foot. Land in a strong stance so that you can continue to defend yourself if necessary.

## The Flying Double Kick

This kick is really two strong front kicks which, used together, make a powerful attack. The flying double kick is used most often to catch an aggressor off guard. Because of its fast, continuous movement, the flying double kick is very difficult to dodge or block.

### Learning Steps

**1.** Start from the modified horse stance, facing the aggressor.

**2.** Throw a strong front kick with your rear leg, jumping forward into the air as you do. This kick is a middle-level kick and should strike the aggressor in the chest, stomach, or solar plexus. Change legs in mid-air and throw another, higher front kick. This kick is an upper-level kick and should hit the aggressor in the head or neck. With each kick, hit the aggressor with the ball of your foot. The kicks will be powerful if you snap your knees when kicking.

**3.** After kicking, be sure to end in any strong fighting stance so that you can continue to defend yourself if necessary.

## The Back-Spinning Circle Kick

This is one of the most powerful kicks in foot fighting. Because of its unique delivery, the kick usually catches an aggressor off guard.

### Learning Steps

**1.** Start from the horse stance, with the side of your body facing the aggressor.

**2.** Pivot on your front foot and swing your body backward toward the aggressor. As you move, continue to look back over your shoulder in the direction your body is turning.

**3.** At the same time, swing your rear leg around and upward in a circular motion. Hit the aggressor in the ribs or the head with the *back* of your heel.

# 7.

# THE USE OF THE FEET AND LEGS FOR THROWING

Like kicks, leg throws and foot sweeps are effective foot-fighting techniques. They cannot be done properly, however, without the use of hand techniques. For this reason, throwing techniques should be practiced with attention to coordinating both hand and foot movements.

It is best to practice leg throws and foot sweeps with a partner. When working with a partner, certain safety precautions should be taken to avoid injury. These precautions include

—being certain that your partner is ready before you execute a throw or sweep.

—limiting the amount of force you exert in executing the technique.

—practicing the throws and sweeps on a thick mat.

## THE BASIC FOOT SWEEP

The basic foot sweep is an excellent self-defense technique for catching an aggressor off guard. The sweep is used most often as a counterattack against an attempted throw. The basic foot sweep can be modified for use in many different fighting situations.

### Learning Steps

**1.** If the aggressor steps forward with his or her right foot, move your left foot to the outside of it.

**2.** Then, using the sole of your foot, sweep the aggressor's foot directly to the side so that he or she is thrown off balance. (Reverse the moves if the aggressor advances with the left foot.) At the same time, get a firm grip on the aggressor's arms and pull them downward to complete the fall.

NOTE: Proper timing is the key to success in sweeping and throwing. This sweep should be practiced many times in order to develop fast reflexes and a sense of timing.

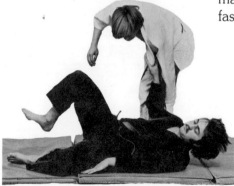

## THE OUTSIDE LEG THROW

The outside leg throw can be used in a variety of self-defense situations. But it is especially useful when the aggressor is standing close to you.

### Learning Steps

**1.** As the attacker grabs you, step forward and place your left foot next to and outside of the attacker's right foot. At the same time, push the person's body backward with your right hand and pull the right arm downward with your left hand.

**2.** Then, slip your right leg around and behind the attacker's right leg so that your thighs are together.

**3.** As you continue to push your opponent backward, kick your right leg straight back and sweep the attacker's leg out from under him or her.

# THE INSIDE LEG THROW

Like the outside leg throw, the inside leg throw can be used when an aggressor is standing very close to you.

### Learning Steps

**1.** Grab the attacker's arms and place your left foot next to and inside of the attacker's right foot. Push the person backward so that his or her balance is broken to the rear.

**2.** As you push, hook your right leg around the aggressor's left leg and kick straight back, pulling the aggressor's leg out from under him or her.

# SAFETY RULES

Proper safety precautions must always be taken when you practice foot-fighting techniques. The important thing to remember is that a practice session is not the same as an actual fight. A practice session is a time when students can work together to improve their self-defense skills. The following list of safety rules has been developed to reduce the risk of personal injury during practice sessions.

**1.** Be sure to do the warm-up exercises before each practice session.

**2.** Do not stretch your muscles too much at any given time. It is better to do a little stretching each day and improve slowly than to do too much all at once and injure your muscles.

**3.** *Do not actually kick your partner.* Stop your kick at least one inch (2.5 centimeters) from your partner's body. To practice the *impact* of your kick, use a punching bag.

**4.** Never surprise your partner with a throw or sweep. Be sure that he or she is ready before you start practicing those techniques.

**5.** Do not practice throws or sweeps with a partner who does not know how to fall properly.

**6.** Always practice throws and sweeps on a thick mat.

# INDEX

## ABOUT THE AUTHOR

Fred Neff has been a student of the Asian fighting arts for most of his life. He started his training at the age of eight and eventually specialized in karate. Today Mr. Neff holds the rank of fifth degree black belt in that fighting art. In addition to karate, he is also proficient in judo and jujitsu. For many years, Mr. Neff has used his knowledge of the Asian fighting arts to educate others. He has taught karate at the University of Minnesota, the University of Wisconsin, and Hamline University and Inver Hills College in St. Paul, Minnesota. He has also organized and supervised self-defense classes in public schools, private schools, and in city recreation departments. Included in his teaching program have been classes for law enforcement officers.

Fred Neff graduated with high distinction from the University of Minnesota College of Education in 1970. In 1976, he received his J.D. degree from William Mitchell College of Law in St. Paul, Minnesota. Mr. Neff is now a practicing attorney in Minneapolis, Minnesota.